LTLYG

Loving God with
heart, soul, mind, & strength.

by Jim Clark

Copyright © 2012 SPUR Christian Projects
First published 2012
ISBN 978-0-9573261-0-1
SPUR Christian Projects
www.spurprojects.org.uk
hello@spurprojects.org.uk

All rights reserved. No part of this publication may be reproduced, stored in a retrieval system, or transmitted in any form or by any means, electronic, mechanical, photocopying, recording or otherwise, without the prior permission of SPUR Christian Projects.

The right of Jim Clark to be identified as author of this work has been ascerted by him in accordance with the Copyright, Designs and Patents Act 1988.

Unless otherwise stated, all scripture quotations taken from THE HOLY BIBLE, NEW INTERNATIONAL VERSION (Anglicised Edition) Copyright ©1979, 1984, 2011 by Biblica (formerly International Bible Society). Used by permission of Hodder and Stoughton Publishers, Ann Hachette UK company. All rights reserved."

Scripture quotations taken from *THE MESSAGE*. Copyright © by Eugene H. Peterson 1993, 1994, 1995, 1996, 2000, 2001, 2002. Used by permission of NavPress Publishing Group.

Designed by Sarah Clark www.designedbysarah.co.uk
Printed by Bell & Bain Limited

ABOUT JIM –

"I'm the founder of SPUR Christian Projects. I'm married to Kate (for 27 years… eek!!) and I've got two adult children. I've been part of the leadership of my local Baptist Church for around 15 years and I've been active in Christian youth work in various forms for around 20 years through this church. I've spent most of my working career in the life and pensions industry with short forays into the public and voluntary sectors and I'm now seeking to spend the remainder of my career challenging, encouraging and supporting other Christians through SPUR Christian Projects."

ABOUT THIS BOOK –

"This is a challenge that I've had on my heart for some time. Having been on the Christian journey for some 30 years, I hope that this (deliberately) short book gets you thinking about your own journey, how well you love God and what priority you give him in your life. Someone used an explosives metaphor recently (stick with me and try to put those pictures of devastation and carnage out of your head!!), we don't know what charges God has set in our lives and we don't know which detonators will set which charge off. We're simply asked to press a detonator.

As someone who has been known to lob in the odd hand grenade, this book is the detonator that I've been assigned to press… so, with thanks to Kate, Sarah, Jennifer, Jeremy, Kenny, Andy, Eric C, Rebekah, Dave, Fiona and all the encouragers at DBC, here goes!!"

CONTENTS

1. **INTRO** 7

2. **WORDS OF LOVE AND LIFE** 12

3. **LOVE** 25

4. **HEART » BELIEVE** 38

5. **SOUL » WORSHIP** 49

6. **MIND » KNOW** 59

7. **STRENGTH » SERVE** 71

8. **HEART, SOUL, MIND & STRENGTH – GIVE IT ALL** 80

9. **NOT THERE YET?** 86

10. **FINAL CHALLENGE... FOR NOW** 94

BEACH
SAND
FOUNDATION
JOKE
SURPRISE
CHALLENGE

I. INTRO

There was I sitting on a beach in the Canary Islands - not my favourite experience – anything above 25 degrees is uncomfortable for this hardy Scotsman and then there is the torture of slapping on sticky sun cream and the sand… it gets everywhere! Anyway, there I am on the beach, under the shade, t-shirt still on for fear of getting sun burn and watching the world go by. We're on the section of the beach just outside the Sheraton hotel and there are a few wealthy people around – designer labels, iPhones, iPads and remote-controlled toy helicopters (not just one toy helicopter but three – one for granddad, one for dad and one for the boy). There are business calls taking place and deals being done. I'm looking around and I'm wondering what these people build their lives on.

I'm reminded of a joke where three friends are attending the funeral of one of their university friends – he's died prematurely and they've gone to the family home to pay their respects before the funeral service. Their friend is lying in an open casket in the large living room. Each of them steps forward to say their good byes and they gather a few steps beyond the coffin. One of the friends looks back and asks the others what they would like their friends to say on an occasion such as this. The first friend, who is a university professor, says "Well, I hope that people will say that I was a great teacher and that I inspired them, that I taught them great things, that I opened their minds to new thinking and new possibilities." They turned to the second friend, an eminent surgeon "Me… I hope that people say that I was a great surgeon, that I saved many lives and improved the quality of life for many people." Finally, it was the third friend's turn and he said "If I'm lying in an open casket like that and people are paying their respects, the thing I most want people to say is "He's alive!!!".

Well there I am, sniggering to myself on the beach, thinking about what people might say about me and a beach ball flies passed and a young boy runs to catch it. (Glad to see that he's got a t-shirt on and a cap to protect him from the rays) He picks up the ball and turns round – his t-shirt catches my eye. At first glance, I thought it said "Mission Impossible". Re-focusing, I can see that it says "Mission Accomplished".

That's it, that's what I'd like people to say about me. Even more, that's what I'd like God to say about me when my life on this earth is over. Well done, mission accomplished.

What about you? What about your mission? It might surprise you to know that you have one. God put each of us on this planet with a purpose in mind.

So this short book is about challenging you to get in line with God's mission for your life. I hope and pray that you do find it a challenge but more than that, I hope that you respond to that challenge.

LTLYG – will you accept the mission?

WORDS OF LOVE AND LIFE

TREASURE
LTLYG
FAILURE
WHOLEHEARTED
MISSION
SIMPLE?

2. WORDS OF LOVE AND LIFE

If I was to ask you which words in God's history of love (aka the bible) mean the most to you - which ones grab you, inspire you, fire you up, which ones do you call on when the going gets tough, which ones makes you well up inside with emotion, which ones spur you on - I wonder which words of love and life God has imprinted on your heart and in your mind.

TREASURE IN WORDS

There are many individual verses in the bible that are pretty fundamental to the Christian faith and that mean a lot to many people… rocks that we can stand on when tests and trials come our way and that we can take shelter in, and winds that carry us and push us on and that quicken our feet.

This booklet is about one of those verses but, strangely, I think that I can say that in all the times that I've heard people tell their story of Jesus working in their lives, I can't remember one person give this verse as their significant verse. That's not to say that there isn't anyone and I guess there will be – it's just that I haven't come across them.

LTLYG

LTLYG

And here's the thing – this verse spells out the greatest, most important words of instruction that we need to get a grip of, understand… and follow. And, it is Jesus who is giving this command Jesus says and, well, he should know,

Not only that (and here's the paradox, or the contradiction) it's THE priority commandment, the big GC (Greatest Commandment) but it seems a step too far for us mere humans to master… I'm pretty sure that we all struggle to keep even one part of it for a nano-second, never mind the whole lot, all of the time.

Having said that, does God ever command something which is completely beyond our reach. Something for you to chew over, methinks!

PREPARE TO FAIL

I would go as far to say that the root of man's problem (and woman's) is found in our inability to follow this command and to understand its significance. This command, as with the ten commandments and the rest of the law, acts as a mirror, allowing us to see our inadequacy and our need for a saviour.

In everyone's life record (if there is such a thing), there will be a red cross against this instruction and a stamp marked FAILED. Just to emphasise this point (and get ready for this, this might be, for some, as serious as hearing someone say for the first time that Santa Claus isn't real) you, me, your mum, dad, your pastor, youth pastor, the little old lady that smiles at you every Sunday morning and seems like an angel, even the most holy person in your church will not have been able to keep this commandment completely.

Rest assured though, we may struggle with these things on this side of eternity but, on the other side, we have the promise of being made perfect.

ARE YOU GETTING IT?

If you are a follower of Jesus, you must have a tight handle on these words – they need to be sunk deep into your heart. More than that, these words, if forged in your heart, can be your lifelong mission. Whatever age and stage you are at in your life, wherever you are in your walk of faith, however close you appear to be to God, these words can be the force in your life, powered by the Holy Spirit, to enable you to reflect and repent and to re-commit (or even commit for the first time) and follow Jesus wholeheartedly.

So what is it? See opposite.

You can find it in other places in both the Old and New Testaments (I'll leave it to you to find them) but I've chosen this one in the book of Mark because of two things – the events surrounding Jesus saying these words and the inclusion in this verse of the last words "and with all your strength". More about these later.

In the meantime, I'm referring to it as LTLYG.

"Love The Lord Your God with ALL your HEART, with ALL your SOUL, with ALL your MIND and with ALL your STRENGTH" Mark 12:30

LTLYG   =   LOVE   THE   LORD   YOUR   GOD

GOALS, MISSIONS, OBJECTIVES, TARGETS?

So I wonder what part LTLYG plays in your life.
I think that I can safely assume that many people will have some personal goals of one form or another whether they are explicit or not. Tick the ones on the list that you've got -

- Pass exam, get Uni. place, get job, get promotion ☐
- Get girlfriend/boyfriend (delete as appropriate) ☐
- Get engaged and then married and have kids ☐
- Get house, get bigger house, get "forever" house ☐
- Save for holiday ☐
- Work out a budget... and stick to it ☐
- Pay off credit card, car loan and mortgage ☐
- Make the team ☐
- Climb a mountain ☐
- Pass driving test, buy first car ☐
- Buy better car (the one that gives me some kudos and status). ☐

Sorry to labour the point but the point is that everyone has something that they're aiming for. I wouldn't dismiss any of those goals – it's a good habit to set goals and to give some focus but what about a spiritual goal? Do you have any? Do you have LTLYG as a goal? I didn't but I'm trying to now. It is a commandment that stretches us mere humans the most and, for some, it is so challenging that they would rather not aim for it at all, fearing failure and disappointment. Without doubt, you will fall short of this command, but, if you take LTLYG as your lifelong goal, I'm convinced that you will not regret it and that God will bless you and what you do for him.

SIMPLES!

At one level, the command simply says that you've got to give your all to God. Enough said or "Simples" as the meerkat says. This might be enough for some but, for me (and I might be the thick one here), I want to understand it better and try to see what it means in practice.

Here are my thoughts and reflections, imperfect as they are. Just to set expectations here, I've not studied theology or been theologically trained and I don't have "Rev" in my title. I've read some books but I couldn't be described as an avid reader – I'm just someone who has chewed over these words. I hope and pray that my reflections will be helpful to you. At the very least, I pray that you will be encouraged and challenged to dig deeper into God's word and that you will find your own focus on this verse.

Some of you might note the obvious and deliberate omission of the verse that follows LTLYG. Loving your neighbour as yourself is another verse that you need to get a grip on. It is a big topic on its own and deserving of its own book (and, perhaps, one will follow).

For now, can I say that loving people flows out of loving God? We cannot love people or ourselves in the way that God wants us to love unless we first understand how to love him.

We don't love people in the same way as we love God but we should love people in the light of loving God.

So, this book is about loving God and doing it wholeheartedly.

(Ladies, stick with me on this. This is a bit of a bloke's example but I'm sure that you'll get it.)

One of the highlights of my year is the 6 Nations Rugby Union Championship. It explodes with power, passion and patriotism each February. As a youth, I was a football man, I just didn't get rugby - it just seemed that whoever was the biggest won and not being the bigget guy on any pitch, it wasn't for me. But now? Wow - it's more than brute strength (although there is a lot of that). It is total commitment to the cause, a do or die mentality that demands players to put their bodies on the line and demands clever, quick thinking.

There are bruising tackles, dislocations, fractures, cuts and a season just wouldn't be the same without a player or two being stretchered off. It's the thinking that goes into game plans, tactics, set plays, keeping possession, gaining territory, whether to kick or pass or run, taking into account the opposition's strengths and weaknesses, the pitch condition and the weather.

These guys are at peak condition, trained to the max and moves are rehearsed, rehearsed and rehearsed. And it takes all sorts - tall, short, heavy, lean, fast, quick thinking, patient, tenacious, brave - and, in any one game, every player without exception has a crucial part to play. Hardly anyone walks off the pitch without having spent their all.

What if all of us Christians lived our lives and loved God with the same passion and commitment as these rugby players play their game?

Surely the man who was perfect and undeserving of any harm and who put his body on the line for us, who suffered excruciating pain and death on our behalf, who took our punishment... surely he deserves total commitment from us - heart, soul, mind and strength.

This is what LTLYG means to me……

LOVE

FIRST LOVED US

ACT

SUPREME

ALL

PERSONAL

PERFECT

⁹ This is how God showed his love among us:
He sent his one and only Son into the world
that we might live through him. ¹⁰ This is love:
not that we loved God, but that he loved us and
sent his Son as an atoning sacrifice for our sins.

1 John 4:9-10

3. LOVE

…let's start with love.

"LOVE" THE LORD YOUR GOD

God's creation and God's plan for redemption were acts of love. God is love and he first loved us – see 1 John 4:9-10. There is only good in God. All his words and all his actions are for his glory, and these actions benefit his people in divine love.

If you were to give your very best - the very best of yourself, giving your most precious possession, the thing that you hold most dearly, knowing that, in doing so, there will be pain and suffering and separation, that kind of love represents love at its highest peak… and that peak is way higher than most of us humans will reach in our lifetimes. Here's a challenge for you – list the people in your life that you would die for………

Got that list? OK, good. I guess (hope) that you've listed your family and, at least some friends? Any strangers or enemies on that list? Anyone who has rejected you, humiliated you, hated you, tortured you, anyone who wants to put you to death… we would be those people on Jesus' list but so great was his love that he died for us, all of us, including his enemies.

From a human point of view, I can't imagine anyone wanting to die for someone who has been deliberately, purposefully and excessively cruel to them – can you? Men and women can't do this… but what about God and his son Jesus? It's in their nature to love, to sacrifice and to forgive!

I want to emphasise that love involves action. James 1:22-25 says –

> [22] Do not merely listen to the word, and so deceive yourselves. Do what it says. [23] Anyone who listens to the word but does not do what it says is like someone who looks at his face in a mirror [24] and, after looking at himself, goes

away and immediately forgets what he looks like. [25] But whoever looks intently into the perfect law that gives freedom, and continues in it—not forgetting what they have heard, but doing it—they will be blessed in what they do.

Love is not just a warm, fuzzy feeling or simply an attraction to or infatuation with someone or something, it is not just a desire or an attitude – love has to expressed, it has to provoke action.

So when God commands us to love him and love others, there needs to be evidence of an expression of that love. You and I need to do something - something has to happen. God has demonstrated his love for us – how can/should we demonstrate our love to God in return?

LOVE "THE LORD YOUR GOD"

He is THE LORD. See what Colossians 1:16 says.

"For in him all things were created: things in heaven and on earth, visible and invisible, whether thrones or powers or rulers or authorities; all things have been created through him and for him." Colossians 1:16

(……… WOW……I'm writing this and I have to stop and read this verse again and again!)

LTLYG   =   LOVE   THE   LORD   YOUR   GOD

We all like it when something is done for us, don't we – whether it's a birthday party or even just someone making a cup of tea for us. For just a short time, we feel important.

In terms of importance, it would be an understatement to say that Jesus stands out there on his own with no contender, no-one remotely close to his position and power and glory. He is absolutely above all things – kings, presidents, governments, armies, CEO's, billionaires – he is above them all. None of them can touch his supremacy.

Where does that leave us? Well I hope that it leaves us in awe of him, ready and willing to love, worship, obey and serve him.

He is YOUR GOD – don't miss this… God is personal to you and this creator of all things wants to have a relationship with little, old, small, insignificant you and me. He is for you, not against you. He is not there to spoil your fun and spoil your life, quite the opposite, he wants you to do his will and this place, in his will, is the best place to be, to live out your life and to live it out to the full.

LOVE THE LORD YOUR GOD "WITH ALL OF MY"

Don't you just wish that that word "all" wasn't there? Not only is it there but it is repeated again and again and again. There's a message there, don't you think – it's important… imperative is probably a better word… it's imperative to have a total, complete, holistic and wholehearted commitment to love God. That word also allows us to gauge how well we're doing in loving God but not, I would suggest, to beat ourselves up with but as a spur to keep on loving.

"MY" – it's personal again. Loving God is your responsibility – loving him with what you have (or what he has given you). He made you the way you are, he loves you the way you are – ok, we've all got some rough edges to have knocked off but God has made you totally unique. Embrace that, thank him for that and love him with all your uniqueness.

Also, don't look to others to have your relationship with God, don't live it through others, whether that's a parent, a church leader, a friend or even an author. Yes, observe and learn – learn from both the good and the worthy and those Christians that seem to get it right but also learn from the failings, flaws and weaknesses of others.

And never, never, think that you have nothing to love God with. He doesn't see you that way. He delights in you if you have your hope in him! So, no reason for you to see yourself like that.

> the Lord delights in those who fear him, who
> put their hope in his unfailing love.
>
> Psalm 147:11

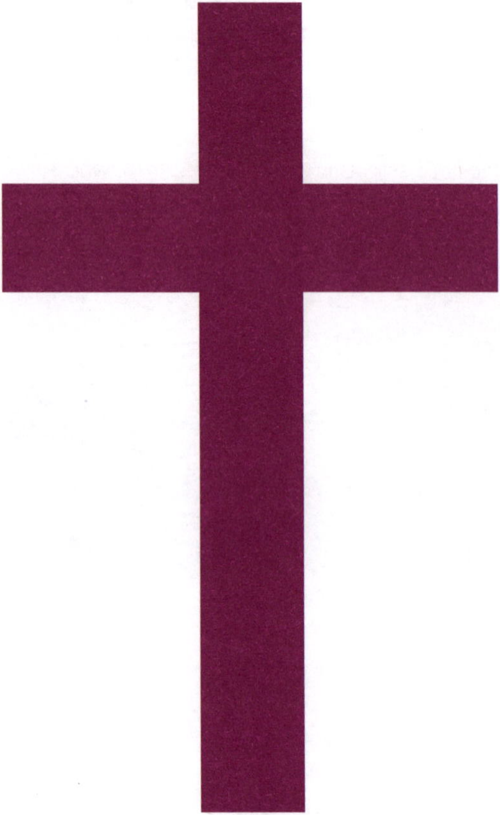

LTLYG = LOVE THE LORD YOUR GOD

JESUS CHRIST – THE PERFECT EXAMPLE

I don't know about you but I'm the kind of person who, if I need to find out how to do something, learns best from seeing someone else do it before I attempt to do it myself. You know what I mean? It's called "see one, do one".

When it comes to being a Christian, we can learn from observing others but there's a clue in the name, Christian, about who it is best to learn from. And that is Jesus.

He is the perfect example of loving God. He loved his father in heaven wholeheartedly. If you've never read a gospel (i.e. Matthew, Mark, Luke or John) from start to finish, why not do that? Take note of Jesus' words and actions and ask yourself whether they're all consistent with someone who loved God. The emphatic answer is yes.

Now, you might say that Jesus was different and it must have been easier for him. After all, he is the son of God and we are mere, limited humans. Surely, he had some kind of superpowers that you and I don't have? Life, here on Earth, some might think, must have been a breeze for him but he was fully human.

Most of us, if we're honest, want an easy life. We set a course in life which, we hope, is straightforward and uncomplicated, one which is free from conflict and trouble, the path of least resistance. Jesus' path certainly wasn't that but he did do normal things, even those normal things that we can struggle with.

Did he have to study and learn the scriptures? Yes – as he is growing up, we find him in the temple engaged with his elders. Did he have to establish a daily discipline of praying to his father? Yes, we find him doing that in the early morning.

Did he get tired? Yes. Was he tempted? Yes. Did he experience sadness and rejection and betrayal and threats on his life? Yes.

You might be thinking that you would have given up. For Jesus, he had much more to come - physical, emotional, mental and spiritual pain in dying on the cross… death and separation from his father. And yet, he still persevered. Did he have some special ability to not feel the pain? No. He did all this out of love for and in obedience to his own father, God.

Heart, soul, mind and strength – he absolutely gave his all. So, if you want to know what love is (I'm sure there's a song in that), get to know Jesus. See what Philippians 2 says about Jesus.

Therefore if you have any encouragement from being united with Christ, if any comfort from his love, if any common sharing in the Spirit, if any tenderness and compassion, ² then make my joy complete by being like-minded, having the same love, being one in spirit and of one mind. ³ Do nothing out of selfish ambition or vain conceit. Rather, in humility value others above yourselves, ⁴ not looking to your own interests but each of you to the interests of the others.

⁵ In your relationships with one another, have the same mindset as Christ Jesus:

⁶ Who, being in very nature God, did not consider equality with God something to be used to his own advantage;⁷ rather, he made himself nothing by taking the very nature of a servant, being made in human likeness. ⁸ And being found in appearance as a man, he humbled himself by becoming obedient to death —
even death on a cross!

Philippians 2:1-8

HEART»
BELIEVE

BELIEVE
PRAY
BELIEVE
WORSHIP
BELIEVE
STUDY
BELIEVE
SERVE

4. HEART » BELIEVE

Romans 10:10 says that it is with our hearts that we believe that Jesus is Lord. OK, it's not the amazing and intricate piece of muscle and tissue that pumps blood around our body that Paul, the writer of Romans, means. It is that intangible "thing" that is at the centre of our being – where our desires, feelings and emotions live. It's the place that determines our behaviour and how we feel about our behaviour and how we respond to other people's behaviours – whether we feel that it is bad or good or indifferent. It gives us our direction, our motivation and courage. It's the place that determines what we believe… and our beliefs shape our thoughts, words and actions.

Robert Murray McCheyne was a young Scottish pastor who lived in 19th century Dundee. He died when he was only 29 but made a mark on many, many people during his life and since. His writings demonstrate a total commitment to Jesus and history confirms the reality of this commitment. He said this about believing -
"Believe nothing, and you will have no joy. Believe little, and you will have little joy. Believe much, and you will have much joy. Believe all, and you will have all joy."

A word about joy - BMW would have you believe that

driving one of their cars is joy. Well it can be a thrill but it only lasts for the first few minutes that you are in the car. Joy is a deep-rooted satisfaction with God and with the life that he gives. Yes, life has it's challenges but believing God is in complete control, whatever comes your way makes a huge difference.

I guess that the obvious question from what McCheyne says is "How much belief do you have?"

DECEIT

It's not all good news though. Jeremiah 17:9 tells us that the heart is deceitful above all things. That is a really interesting word – deceitful… full of deceit, full of lies, dishonesty and pretence. Who is being deceived here? Well, primarily, we're deceiving ourselves. So our hearts deceive us and we think that we're one thing but are really another. We say that we believe one thing but we do the very opposite of what we believe.

So the heart is the very core of our being but is deceitful above all things – that puts us in a pretty hopeless place, doesn't it? Well, we're not a lost cause – Ecclesiastes 3:11 tells us that God has set eternity in our hearts. He has given us a longing, a desire for something beyond what we can see and touch in this world. Ephesians 3:17 says that Jesus may dwell in our hearts through faith. With that desire and with that faith, our hearts can be filled not with deceit but with faith and belief.

JESUS' HEART MISSION

Just in case this point passes you by, I hope that I have been able to get over the fact that the heart is a critical place, the critical place and that it is this part of our being that God addresses through sending his son into this world. God didn't choose to send Jesus into this world to mobilise a military revolution or to impose a new political system or to sort out the world's economy or to fix our physical and mental frailties (although I would argue that all of these have been/can be influenced and directed by God). Jesus was on a mission to repair our hearts, to restore our belief in God and to reconcile us to God.

DO YOU BELIEVE?

So the heart is a pretty important place, more than that it is the important place and God asks us to love him with all of our hearts. He is asking us to believe him, to trust him, to have faith in him, to take him at his word, to believe that

> » This world and this universe was created and is sustained by God
> » God gives you and me life and breath
> » He loves us beyond our understanding,
> » He is intimately interested in our lives and wellbeing
> » Jesus dealt with our sin when he took it upon Himself on the cross, taking our place, taking our punishment
> » Jesus died and came back to life having been dead
> » Jesus is sitting at God's right hand, interceding

for us
» He left his Holy Spirit to guide us
» Jesus is coming back again and that He will rule for eternity
» God listens and responds to our prayers

There is a lot more that could be listed, lot's more. The challenge is not necessarily to list more but to ask ourselves whether we truly believe. Believing is accepting something as true or real. That's the command that is made in LTLYG. Accept what we read and have heard passed down the ages about God and Jesus and the Holy Spirit as true and real.

DOUBTS?

In this information society where we know so much more than ever before, where knowledge is power, where science has made great strides and, in so doing, has shaken our beliefs, God calls us to still believe in him.

He doesn't expect us to do this irrationally or without thought and he doesn't expect us to be able to do it on our own. He sent his Holy Spirit to help so call on him if you're lacking in faith. I'm encouraged by Thomas' predicament in John 20 – he wasn't there when Jesus appeared and he wouldn't believe until he saw Jesus with his own eyes and touched his wounds with his own hands. Jesus re-appeared especially for Thomas. Now, I think that this was a real one-off in the way that Jesus re-appeared but I'm convinced that, when we are doubtful and when we ask for help, God, through his Holy Spirit, sends words, people, events and experiences into our lives to show us that he is real.

Also consider that our hearts deceive and that we have a force working against us, i.e. Satan. All the more, then, we have to ask God for that gift of faith and to exercise it when he gives it to us.

SHOWING OUR BELIEF

How do we demonstrate our belief?

Prayer – talk to God, in Jesus name, about your life, ask him what to do, ask him to act, to intervene, to change things and believe that he will. Ask him to forgive. Pray for others as well.

Worship – thank him and praise him for who he is and for his intervention, involvement and interest in your life. Whatever your circumstances, you can always thank him. Make it a priority to join others to do the same. Make it a habit.

Study – learn more about what God has done in the past for his people. Study his word, listen to and learn from others. It will inspire you, give you faith and courage.

Service - when God tugs at your heart to do something or makes you restless about an issue, be sure to act and do his will, in faith and with wholehearted belief.

That's how we love him with all of our hearts – we believe. That belief will shape our motives, our desires, our thoughts, our words, our actions.

SOUL » WORSHIP

WORSHIP
SING
WORSHIP
LIVE
WORSHIP
OFFER
WORSHIP
KEEP WORSHIPPING

Psalm 103

¹ Praise the Lord, my soul; all my inmost being, praise his holy name.
² Praise the Lord, my soul,
and forget not all his benefits—
³ who forgives all your sins
and heals all your diseases,
⁴ who redeems your life from the pit
and crowns you with love and compassion,
⁵ who satisfies your desires with good things
so that your youth is renewed like the eagle's.
⁶ The Lord works righteousness
and justice for all the oppressed.
⁷ He made known his ways to Moses,
his deeds to the people of Israel:
⁸ The Lord is compassionate and gracious,
slow to anger, abounding in love.
⁹ He will not always accuse,
nor will he harbour his anger forever;
¹⁰ he does not treat us as our sins deserve
or repay us according to our iniquities.
¹¹ For as high as the heavens are above the earth, so great is his love for those who fear him;
¹² as far as the east is from the west, so far has he removed our transgressions from us.
¹³ As a father has compassion on his children,
so the Lord has compassion on those who fear

him;
¹⁴ for he knows how we are formed,
he remembers that we are dust.
¹⁵ The life of mortals is like grass,
they flourish like a flower of the field;
¹⁶ the wind blows over it and it is gone,
and its place remembers it no more.
¹⁷ But from everlasting to everlasting
the Lord's love is with those who fear him, and
his righteousness with their children's
children —
¹⁸ with those who keep his covenant
and remember to obey his precepts.
¹⁹ The Lord has established his throne in heaven,
and his kingdom rules over all.
²⁰ Praise the Lord, you his angels, you mighty
ones who do his bidding, who obey his word.
²¹ Praise the Lord, all his heavenly hosts,
you his servants who do his will.
²² Praise the Lord, all his works
everywhere in his dominion.

Praise the Lord, my soul.

5. SOUL » WORSHIP

Before going any further, take some time out to read Psalm 103. Dwell on it for a few minutes and consider who God really is and what he has done for you and me. Read each sentence a couple of times, if you need to – let it sink into your heart and mind. Let it touch your soul.

I hope and pray that your response to that Psalm is praise and worship to God. We serve a wonderful, amazing God… it's our souls that worship him, isn't it? Our hearts believe and our souls worship.

And, isn't it our souls that are saved? And isn't it our souls that will worship God in heaven for eternity?

SINGING WORSHIP

I don't know what you think of worship. I'm of the age that I can remember singing hymns and saying the Lord's prayer every day at primary school – it was a chore, sorry to say especially when we had to learn some hymns for school church services. We were not a church going family when I was growing up but I went to Sunday School for a while so it wasn't all foreign to me when I started going to a small Baptist church in my teens. (Before I sound too spiritual, I only went because I really liked one of the girls!)

What struck me though was the way in which these people were singing their hearts out. It wasn't the kind of congregation that did a lot of raising their hands, etc but, looking at and hearing some of those people, you could tell that they were worshipping a God that they loved. Is that the kind of worship that you bring?

And on this subject of worshipping together, don't be numbered among those who don't make it a priority to be at church, meeting and enjoying fellowship with his people and with him. We all miss out when people absent themselves from church – we are all much poorer, especially when young people and families decide that it's not for them.

I suppose that's what most of us think of first when considering what worship is – singing in church. Of course, loving God with all our souls is much more than this – it's what we say to God, it's how we say it, it's how we involve God in our lives. Dare I say that it is even about the time that we give to being in God's presence? I like the explanation that worship is what we give worth to.

LIVING WORSHIP

God calls us to give worth to him, to take time out, to turn to him and tell him what he means to us. This is a daily duty…

You worship when you

- take time to talk to God and tell him how much you love him before rushing in to the day.
- thank him for another day to live and breathe, for your health, for a roof over your head, for food on your table and clothes on your back.
- ask him what he would have you do today, how you should use your opportunities and your possessions
- seek his direction for the big and not so big decisions in your life, in your relationships, in your career choices.

- do your best at school, uni or work, when you are kind to others, when you give to others, when you do his will.

Our whole lives are about worship and giving glory to God. Put God first, give him his rightful place. Each day is for his glory, for his will to be done.

Quite a few years ago, I met a lovely lady in a nursing home. We were there to sing carols - to be honest everyone else was singing and I was droning quietly, as I do. She really enjoyed the little sing song and, as we got talking afterwards, she told me a few things about her life and the changes that she had seen in her almost 90 years. She explained about one constant though, one thing that hadn't changed and put it something like this "Talking to God is my first and last duty. For as long as I can remember, that's been my practice. You've got to start and end the day with the Lord".

Perhaps, you don't like the thought of duty but she was spot on with that practice. Starting and ending the day with the Lord... something that we should all aim for.

READY AND AVAILABLE

Romans 12:1-2 gives us direction on this topic of worship.

Roman 12:1-2

Therefore, I urge you, brothers and sisters, in view of God's mercy, to offer your bodies as a living sacrifice, holy and pleasing to God—this is your true and proper worship. ² Do not conform to the pattern of this world, but be transformed by the renewing of your mind. Then you will be able to test and approve what God's will is — his good, pleasing and perfect will.

LTLYG = LOVE THE LORD YOUR GOD

Knowing God is the goal - really knowing. When was the last time that you did a multiple choice test? If you're anything like me (and shame on you if you are!), you might not have done all the study needed or read all the books before the test. Perhaps, you've taken the risky approach of doing just enough to pass. Some questions you know the answer to, some you don't and some you're unsure of. Have you ever guessed at the answers and, by some miracle, got them right? Everyone thinks that you're well brainy, that you know your stuff but the truth is that you don't really. You might have achieved a good score but that isn't a true reflection of what you really know.

Some of us might think that we know celebrities that we see on stage, on film and on TV, especially with so-called reality TV series . But unless we know these people personally, i.e. we've spent a lot of time with them, talking to them, listening to their hearts, we don't really know them. And it is highly improbable that we'll ever get that opportunity.

With God, he doesn't want you to have a limited head knowledge of himself - he has given his word, sent his son into the world and given his Holy Spirit - he wants you to have a close relationship, closer than a friend or brother or sister. He is available 24/7/365 for you to get to know him.

We are challenged to offer ourselves – it's our spiritual act of worship. If you've never done this, I urge you to do it – make yourself available to do God's will. It will not be without it's challenges but he won't let you down.

Don't underestimate the challenges (or the blessings for that matter) – we're talking about changing our lifestyles here and we can be pretty protective and resistant to change. But we can't love God with all our souls without changing. God is not going to barge into our lives. We need to make time and space for him, and allow his Holy Spirit free rein to mould us and equip us, and to change our thinking, our attitudes, our desires and our circumstances. We need to let go of those things that hold us back from being available to him and that prevent us from worshipping him.

This could be as simple as setting the alarm clock a little earlier or changing your Sunday timetable. It might be major though – do your friends distract you from God? What about your job? What about your finances – have you ever said that you can't afford to do what God is asking? And what about the gifts and talents that God has given you - are you making them available back to him?

Be ready. Be available.

WHEN IT'S TOUGH GOING

No doubt there will be times when you and I don't feel like worshipping, praying, singing, being with other Christians - perhaps because of sin, or a disappointment, a hurt, an illness, maybe? Worship isn't primarily about us, though, is it? It's about God, it's about lifting up the name of Jesus.

Space doesn't permit me to share my experiences. Suffice to say that in most of the tough experiences I have had, I sense that Jesus, through his Holy Spirit, is closer. Closer because he wants to help, to restore, to build up and, when necessary, yes, to correct me. He understands all our downsides. He isn't surprised or shocked by what we do or how we feel - he just knows.

So next time, when you don't feel like being in God's presence, why don't you remind yourself of Psalm 103 and approach him with boldness, humility and thankfulness? He will not disappoint you.

MIND»
KNOW

KNOW
READ
CHOOSE WISDOM
KNOW
STRETCH YOUR MIND
GUARD YOUR MIND
KNOW
CHRIST'S MIND
MAX YOUR MIND

6. MIND » KNOW

I'm no expert but the little I know tells me that the human mind is one of the most, if not the most, complex entities in all of creation. Your mind is totally unique to you.

What you think is utterly confidential – no other human knows what you think, unless you disclose it to them. No one knows what I think. People can guess or perhaps attempt to work it out by what we say or do but even in that, we can be pretty good at covering up our thoughts.

Having said that, there is someone who is intimately familiar with our thoughts and that is God. He knows what we think. He knows our hopes, fears, joys, struggles and stresses, desires, likes and dislikes, feelings towards others – he knows.

He knows that our minds can be an instrument for good but also for harm. Think of the things that we do with our minds – we think, we question, we study, we analyse, we learn, we digest, we filter, we decide, we accept, we reject, we change our minds and we make up our minds.

It is the faculty that we use to get to know God. And it is also one of Satan's main battlefields to thwart a Christian engaging with God. It's an important place!

READ THE BOOK!!

Do you know that saying "it goes without saying" – the irony is that the thing that they're referring to and that goes without saying and is obvious, well that thing is usually the very thing that is necessary to say. So, it goes without saying, that you need to read God's word, study God's word and hear people teaching from God's word to learn from it and understand it.

I know that there are miraculous stories of bibles stopping bullets and preventing deaths but simply having a bible in your possession doesn't endow you with any special knowledge or power. A bible is no good if it only sits on a bookshelf, on your bedside table or as an unopened icon on your smartphone… you have to open it and read it!

Apologies for that little rant – it is obvious though, isn't it but, if you were to ask any mature Christian, I'm pretty sure every single one would say that it is not always easy going trying to establish and maintain that discipline of reading God's word – Satan doesn't want you to read God's word and he'll do anything in his power to prevent you from picking it up.

Reading God's word is the start of the journey from belief to knowledge.

WISE OR STUPID – YOU CHOOSE!

> Ecclesiastes 10:2 in the Message says
> "Wise thinking leads to right living: Stupid thinking leads to wrong living."

Do you want to be a wise thinker or a stupid thinker? Daft question, isn't it?

Take time out to read some verses from Proverbs 2 and 3 below… Hold on. Wait. You'll only get the benefit of reading this if you have a mind that is willing and open to being taught by the Spirit. Have you got that kind of mind or is your mind already made up? Why don't you ask God to give you the kind of mind that will soak up his word, that will treasure his word and that will even memorise his word.

OK, now read (if you've got a bible read the whole of both the chapters) and you'll find that it says that wisdom, understanding, discretion, knowledge of God is essential to living for God and loving God.

So, reading and studying God's word is pretty fundamental to being able to love God with our minds, as is having the right attitude. Apply your mind to getting to know God through his word.

Proverbs 2

My son, if you accept my words and store up my commands within you, ² turning your ear to wisdom and applying your heart to understanding — ³ indeed, if you call out for insight and cry aloud for understanding, ⁴ and if you look for it as for silver and search for it as for hidden treasure, ⁵ then you will understand the fear of the Lord and find the knowledge of God. ⁶ For the Lord gives wisdom; from his mouth come knowledge and understanding.

Proverbs 3

⁵ Trust in the Lord with all your heart and lean not on your own understanding; ⁶ in all your ways submit to him, and he will make your paths straight. ⁷ Do not be wise in your own eyes; fear the Lord and shun evil.

Proverbs 3

¹³ Blessed are those who find wisdom, those who gain understanding, ¹⁴ for she is more profitable than silver and yields better returns than gold.

¹⁵ She is more precious than rubies; nothing you desire can compare with her.

¹⁶ Long life is in her right hand; in her left hand are riches and honour.

¹⁷ Her ways are pleasant ways, and all her paths are peace.

¹⁸ She is a tree of life to those who take hold of her; those who hold her fast will be blessed.

¹⁹ By wisdom the Lord laid the earth's foundations, by understanding he set the heavens in place;

²⁰ by his knowledge the watery depths were divided, and the clouds let drop the dew.

²¹ My son, do not let wisdom and understanding out of your sight, preserve sound judgment and discretion; ²² they will be life for you, an ornament to grace your neck.

²³ Then you will go on your way in safety, and your foot will not stumble.

³⁵ The wise inherit honour, but fools get only shame.

STRETCH YOUR MIND

OK we've established that we've got to read the book and that there is good reason to. Here's another paradox – the main truths in God's word are easy to grasp but the bible's teachings stretch even the most intelligent minds.

Consider that tens of thousands, if not hundreds of thousands, of books have been written trying to explain what the bible tells us.

Consider the challenge to understand how the whole bible works together… history, law, poetry, instruction, prophecy… and how God's perfect will is played out through vastly different characters and, in some cases, very surprising events.

Think about the challenge to apply what the bible teaches to this ever changing world. Think about today's moral and ethical issues and how God's word can guide us.

The bible tells us that God's ways are perfect! Is this just down to having faith or is it actually possible to know God's word well enough to logically prove that this is the case? I'd suggest the latter. There's a challenge for you – apply your mind to discovering God's perfect ways!

THE MIND OF CHRIST

But it is more than this, surely we seek to know the mind of Christ?

> for, "Who has known the mind of the Lord so as to instruct him?" But we have the mind of Christ.
> 1 Cor 2:16

Reading God's word and studying it is a start. Praying, talking to him and listening to him gives us insight into the mind of Christ. There is the promise that if we ask, seek or knock God will satisfy our appetite.

I read a book recently by Bill Hybels entitled The Power of a Whisper – Hearing God and Having the Guts to Respond. It reinforced that God talks to us in all sorts of ways – through his word, in prayer, through other people, through events. The question is whether we are listening and willing to respond.

You've heard that we've got two ears and one mouth, haven't you, suggesting that we should do more listening than talking. Peter, in his first book, encourages us to be alert (and sober), twice. Keep your eyes and ears open to what God is showing and telling you.

Apply your mind to listening to God.

GUARD YOUR MIND

The bible uses these words to describe states of mind that we can be in - troubled, confused, anxious, closed, warped, deluded, disturbed, poisoned, depraved, dull, blinded, corrupt.

Don't sound good, do they? I don't know what you think that you can cope with in your mind but our thoughts are heavily influenced by what we read, watch, listen to and experience. For the follower of Christ, there is so much that is freely available and easily accessible now that can harm our minds and it takes a pretty special person to be unaffected by it. Be careful out there!

Have a look at Philippians 4:7 and ask God to guard your heart and mind in Christ Jesus.

> And the peace of God, which transcends all understanding, will guard your hearts and your minds in Christ Jesus.
>
> Philippians 4:7

How we think can be influenced by other people as well – family, friends, classmates, workmates… and it's not always a healthy influence. How can we counter that? See Philippians 4:8 – it would be worth memorising this verse.

> Finally, brothers and sisters, whatever is true, whatever is noble, whatever is right, whatever is pure, whatever is lovely, whatever is admirable—if anything is excellent or praiseworthy—think about such things.
> Philippians 4:8

Apply your mind to what is true, noble, right, pure, lovely, admirable, excellent and praiseworthy.

Some other words that the bible uses for states of mind - keen, steadfast, right, open, free, willing, alert, sober. That's more like the kind of mind that I want and need. That's a mind that is governed by the Spirit (Romans 8:6).

> The mind governed by the flesh is death, but the mind governed by the Spirit is life and peace.
> Romans 8:6

IN EVERY AREA OF OUR LIVES

God wants us to do our best in every area of our llives. That means taking advantage of every opportunity to learn – whether that's at school, at home, at uni, in work. This might be a struggle for some but stick to it and you'll get your reward. You see God wants Christians who are great Christians but also who are great husbands, wives, mums, dads, sons and daughters, who are great friends, co-workers and team mates. He wants Christians who are great social workers, web developers, bus drivers, architects, doctors, car mechanics, project managers, engineers, bankers, joiners, plumbers, shop workers, scientists or whatever he is giving you the opportunity to do.

Think of the big challenges and issues we still face in hunger, disease, social injustices, sharing the world's resources, war, ethics, politics and where there is strife and conflict between peoples. Think of those smaller, but still significant, challenges that we face in our daily lives, e.g. relationship and money problems. God wants people who know him, his word, *and* who are experts in their fields to be involved in resolving those issues.

God has given us all different gifts and talents, whatever our mental capacity – he wants us to use it to the max.

STRENGTH
»SERVE

STRENGTH
JOSHUA
MOSES
STRENGTH
DAVID
PAUL
STRENGTH
PETER

7. STRENGTH » SERVE

I mentioned at the start that I was referring to the version of the greatest commandment in Mark because it included this last aspect of loving God with all our strength.

It is very easy, and, perhaps for some, desirable to live a Christian life which is completely internal, doesn't disturb you, me or anyone else and has no obvious evidence of life other than, perhaps, attending church once a week or less.

I read of the great servants of God in the bible, Moses, Joshua, David, Paul, Peter, for example, and I see in them, not just a passion for God but a passion for doing his will. I see from James2:14 a clear explanation that faith and deeds are inseparable.

I reflect on Jesus, the servant King, and can only conclude and say "Amen" to the truth that we are his hands and feet, we are his voice, we are his ambassadors to this world.

And we need strength to serve him – whether that is physical strength, mental strength, spiritual strength or moral strength.

James 2:14

What good is it, my brothers and sisters, if someone claims to have faith but has no deeds? Can such faith save them?

STRENGTH TO STICK CLOSE TO GOD'S WORD

I love the account of Joshua – he was one of the 12 who ventured into the Promised Land and was one of the 2 whose advice was rejected, yet he stayed the course for 40 years in the wilderness to become the leader of the Israelites after Moses died. He led them across a parted Jordan and captured Jericho and won many, many, battles.

As a military leader, he would have been physically strong but it is fascinating to read in Joshua 1 that when God tells him to be bold and strong, God doesn't then give some advice to pump some more iron or to do a few more press-ups. He tells Joshua to obey his commandments and to keep his, i.e. God's, law on his lips, meditating on it day and night. God also gives Joshua a promise that he will be with him wherever Joshua went.

So Joshua's strength was required to obey God's law, to keep it on his lips and to keep meditating on it. It's the same for us today. We may not be fighting physical battles but we are fighting daily battles to do God's will. Whether it is opening your bible, kneeling to pray, recalling God's word at a time of need or serving him, Satan wants to mix it with us. Ask God for strength to resist his distractions and temptations.

STRENGTH TO SERVE

Another time out! Read Philippians 2 again. Selfish? Conceited? Looking to your own interests? Grumbling and arguing? Would we be described like this?
Or would we be described as someone who shows humility, values others above ourselves, looks to the interest of others and has the same mind set as that of Jesus?

Jesus – he humbled himself, took the nature of a servant and was obedient to death. Paul, Timothy and Epaphroditus all seemed to get this. They all modelled themselves on Jesus and were prepared to put their lives on the line, not for their own personal glory but because they knew how critical it was/is to let people know who Jesus was and what he had done for them. And what did Paul say about Timothy in particular – he was someone who genuinely cared about others and had proved himself.

It's fascinating – God will give us opportunities to prove ourselves. He'll start small with us and, as we handle the small things, he'll give us bigger and more demanding things to do. He is absolutely on our side and wants us to succeed.

NOT JUST IN CHURCH!

Most of us spend most of our time and energy doing stuff that isn't "sacred", i.e. isn't directly related to church life… whether that's at school, at uni or college, in work, at home or at leisure. That shouldn't give us any reason not to apply this command of loving God with all our strength to all areas of our lives.

In fact, even more so… we are ambassadors of Christ, wherever we are and whatever we do. Colossians 3:23 says that we should work at whatever we do with all our hearts, as if we were working for the Lord and not for human masters.

So whether you're in the classroom, living room, factory, office, gym or on the pitch, put your all into it.

STRENGTH TO TAKE FAITH STEPS AND TO PERSEVERE

Remember earlier, I referred to Romans 12:1-2 – we need to make ourselves available to God and then his will is revealed to us. Joshua knew what God's will was. We can as well – whether it is what to do with our day or what to do with our lives. If we make ourselves available with a servant attitude, he will guide us and direct us.

We will need strength to take those first steps of faith, to serve others' interests (and not our own). We will need strength to stay on the course.

I have to tell you that it has taken a long time for me to get to this point of launching on this different path with God. Despite the many times that God has put these thoughts in my heart and mind, despite challenges and opportunities to respond and to do his will and despite barriers being removed and objections being dismissed, it has taken a bit of a push from God through circumstances that were not entirely within my control.

Don't underestimate your own resistance to doing God's will. Don't underestimate the pull of the world's attractions and the attraction of doing something else. Don't underestimate your capacity for thinking that it is all going to turn out bad and that you'll fail, so it's best not to start at all. Don't underestimate Satan's opposition.

In those times of doubt and opposition and lack of success, be strong and persevere – turn to God for help. Remember that God is with you through his Holy Spirit, just as he was with Joshua.

HEART
SOUL
MIND
STRENGTH
— GIVE
IT ALL

BELIEVE
WORSHIP
KNOW
SERVE

8. HEART, SOUL, MIND & STRENGTH – GIVE IT ALL

OK, there is a lot of overlap between heart, soul, mind and strength. (As I said, this way of thinking about the greatest commandment has helped me, it may not provide all the answers but I hope and pray that it helps you.)

Our beliefs prompt worship, God reveals himself and speaks to us in our worship. This reinforces our beliefs and increases our knowledge. Our beliefs prompt us to learn more and as we learn more our knowledge increases, as does our worship and this again reinforces our beliefs. When we serve him, we experience him at work, we see him change circumstances and lives, we see him bless, we learn more of his ways. Our belief and faith is increased, we worship and our hearts are challenged to serve him more.

We could describe it as a virtuous cycle – each step builds on the previous one and you get more and more positive results. The overwhelming message though is that all four - heart, soul, mind and strength - should be aligned to God's will.

In all that I've tried to convey, I want to emphasise at this point that we can do nothing apart from God, or, in other words, we need to be connected to God, in tune with him. Loving him with all our hearts, souls, minds and strength doesn't come from us just trying hard, however commendable that might be. We need his help and his Holy Spirit's empowering to love him wholeheartedly.

Loving God in His strength, with His Spirit, for His glory. and knowing that He first loved us…. what about you? Are you up for this?

If you're like me, perhaps, you haven't loved God as well as you could. The good news is that you can start doing something about that today. I pray that you will.

Take that bold step, turn to him and tell him that you're sorry for not loving him wholeheartedly. Commit your way to him again, now. Make LTLYG your goal, your mission. Tell him that you're available to do his will and that you want to

- believe in him with all your heart
- worship him with all your soul
- know him with all your mind
- serve him with all your strength

God the Father, his son Jesus and the Holy Spirit will not let you down.

PRACTICAL STEPS TO TAKE

Here are just a few practical steps that you can take –

1. Why don't you find someone who can help you... a pastor, a youth pastor, another church leader, a Christian with more miles on the clock?
2. Write down your commitment to believe, worship, know and serve.
3. Write down what you believe. List the things that you are unsure of and find someone (see above) to help you through them.
4. Make it a priority to connect with God every day
5. Make it a priority to connect with God's people at least once per week.
6. Get ready for worship – get right with God.
7. Hook up to a study group.
8. Write down your prayers... and answers to prayers.
9. Tell others about how God is working in your life.
10. Find a job at church or in your church community.
11. Ask God what he wants you to do with your life.

Of course, you may have done or be doing some of this already. You may have other things that you're doing as well. Great – why don't you share what you're doing with someone else?

NOT THERE YET?

GOD'S LOVE
OUR REJECTION
LOVE
JUSTICE
MERCY
BELIEVE?
DECIDE
BELIEVE!

[28] One of the teachers of the law came and heard them debating. Noticing that Jesus had given them a good answer, he asked him, "Of all the commandments, which is the most important?"
[29] "The most important one," answered Jesus, "is this: 'Hear, O Israel: The Lord our God, the Lord is one.[30] Love the Lord your God with all your heart and with all your soul and with all your mind and with all your strength.'[31] The second is this: 'Love your neighbour as yourself.' There is no commandment greater than these."
[32] "Well said, teacher," the man replied. "You are right in saying that God is one and there is no other but him. [33] To love him with all your heart, with all your understanding and with all your strength, and to love your neighbour as yourself is more important than all burnt offerings and sacrifices."
[34] When Jesus saw that he had answered wisely, he said to him, "You are not far from the kingdom of God." And from then on no one dared ask him any more questions.

Mark 12:28-34

9. NOT THERE YET?

A word for those of you who are not yet followers of Jesus or not yet Christians, who are not yet believers. Whether you are a seeker, a sceptic, an atheist, an agnostic – however you might describe yourself or be described by others, it's important for you to understand the significance of not heeding these words.

GOD'S LOVE – OUR REJECTION

When God created this world and human beings, it was an act of love on his part – that reminds me, his word tells us that he loved us first. It was his desire to live with us, in peace. There was a condition, a very important one that God set out to Adam and Eve, and it was one that they rejected and failed to keep. In some ways, the detail of the condition wasn't important – it was the fact that they were to keep to it but didn't that was significant. They failed to respond in love by keeping God's command and, if it hasn't struck you before, God, as creator, was and is entitled to give commands.

Failure to keep his commands, failure to love him and obey him is what we know of as sin and sin separates us from God. Sin, if we don't do anything about it, ultimately condemns us to an eternity without God. God cannot have sin in his presence – this could leave us without hope because we humans are absolutely incapable of doing anything about this sin ourselves. Yes, we can express sorrow for what we've done but we would find it impossible to make complete amends for our sin and not to sin again. That's why I say that we can't keep this command all the time.

LOVE, JUSTICE AND MERCY

But, God is still the God of love and the God of justice. There was a wrongdoing and that wrongdoing or debt had to be paid for? We couldn't pay it so God himself, in the person of his Son dying on a cross, paid that debt for us. Another awesome act of love!

Just to emphasise this, it's like owing someone money and the person who you owe the money to goes into his own personal bank account to pay off your debt in full. Or it's like you've committed a crime and the person that you've committed the crime against decides to serve your prison term for you. This is what the bible describes as mercy… and mercy is born out of love.

Historians, whether they are Christians or not, and even teachers from other faiths will tell you that the man called Jesus, the one described in the bible, lived around 2000 years ago. He did many amazing things during his life. They will tell you that this man's life and death has impacted our world more than any other person or group of people and more than any other event – there is no question about that and that impact goes on. Jesus was (and is) real. He himself claimed to be the son of God and, well, when I read the bible, I see that Jesus was doing the kind of stuff that I'd expect the son of God to be doing.

I BELIEVE. AND YOU?

Don't forget Jesus was in a tomb for three days and on the third day he rose back to life. Incredible! Unbelievable? No, definitely believable! I believe that God created this world and universe – it's not too much of a stretch to then believe that he could raise someone from the dead (that's not to suggest that it was a minor or easy job!).

To be honest, I don't quite get it all and I would rather have it another way. I'd rather that God's solution to our problem didn't involve his own son being horribly killed BUT that is his way. I see how it all fits together – his creation – our sin – our incapacity - his solution – his payment – his love and mercy – his glory. I believe, I accept it all to be true and because I've told him that I'm sorry and that I believe this, I am forgiven for my sin. I'm forgiven for all the times that I've chosen not to go God's way, not to do God's will, for the times that I've ignored him and not allowed him into my life, for the times that I've not loved him.

What do I get out of this "deal"? Well, I get what I don't deserve (that's called grace) - I get someone who stands by me, whatever the circumstances, I get someone who knows exactly what I go through, who knows the temptations, the sorrows, the hurt, the betrayal — I get a real, true, honest, loving friend. I get someone who guides, who wants the best for me, who keeps me on the straight path, who gives me new purpose and shows me how to live life to the full. I get love and joy and peace and a whole lot more.

> But the fruit of the Spirit is love, joy,
> peace, forbearance, kindness, goodness,
> faithfulness, [23] gentleness and self-control.
> Against such things there is no law.
>
> Galatians 5:22-23

I get a new life… and, of course, there is that small matter of getting to spend eternity with God, as well!

What about you?

(Quick reality check. Don't get me wrong, being a

Christian has its benefits and blessings but it can be tough. If you're someone who wants a comfortable life, who wants to take the path of least resistance then think carefully.)

In Mark 12:28-34, Jesus is challenged by someone who might have been trying to trip him up. He's asked the question, "Which commandment is the most important?" Of course, Jesus answers correctly and with the following

> "Love The Lord Your God with ALL your HEART, with ALL your SOUL, with ALL your MIND and with ALL your STRENGTH".

There's then a short exchange confirming that Jesus and his questioner were in agreement and, then, Jesus says something really significant – he says to his inquisitor "You are not far from the kingdom of heaven."

Can I encourage you by highlighting that the fact that you're reading this, I would suggest, shows that you are searching and that God is drawing you closer to his kingdom. I pray that God will reveal to you that these words are true.

DECISION

So who is he to you?

Do you think that he was a deluded but very, persuasive and powerful person? Was he a bit of a magician, a conjurer? Was he just a really good bloke?
Or could he be who he himself claimed to be… the son of God?

John 11 tells how Lazarus, a good friend of Jesus, died. To reassure and challenge Martha (Lazarus' sister), Jesus says to her, 'I am the resurrection and the life. The one who believes in me will live, even though they die; and whoever lives by believing in me will never die. Do you believe this?'

Jesus says the very same to you and asks the very same question.

Do you believe that Jesus is the son of God? Do you believe that he died in your place to take your punishment and to deal with your sin? Do you believe that he rose again and that he is alive today?

Before you answer those questions, do me one favour… close your eyes, ask God to show you who Jesus is. Take your time to listen to what God is saying to you.

If you're believing this (and I pray that God has opened your eyes to this) – you need to be telling him that you're sorry. Just close your eyes and tell him out loud or tell him silently in your head, tell him that you're sorry for not loving him, for excluding him from your life, for ignoring him, for doing stuff that he didn't want you to do, for not doing stuff that he did want you to do. Tell him you want to change your ways. Tell him that you want to follow Jesus.

If you've told him all this, tell someone else – tell someone that you trust. Find someone to celebrate with you, to support you and to encourage you.

If you're still unsure and perhaps you've still got questions, whatever you do, please, please, please don't stop asking those questions. Keep asking God, keep asking your pastor, youth pastor, church leaders or your Christian friends.

FINAL CHALLENGE ...FOR NOW

10. FINAL CHALLENGE… FOR NOW

A final challenge from me, for now. Let's remind ourselves of those rugby players - totally committed, in peak condition, trained and rehearsed to the max, putting their bodies on the line… and it's just a game!

Hold on, it's really just a game - yes, of course, they take it seriously, and so do I when my team loses BUT it's not a game we're in. It really is about life and death - eternal life.

Perhaps, a better example is the example of the army Put aside any views on whether we should be fighting wars for a moment. I've never served in this way but I know that it isn't a game for them when bullets are flying past their heads, when IED's are exploding around them and when they stand at gravesides saying farewell to their comrades, knowing that it could have been them.

Dedication, discipline, obedience, commitment, expertise, bravery, boldness, belief in their comrades and their leaders, pride, intelligence, spirit, self-control, perseverance, endurance, resolve - that's what it takes to fight in a battle. These guys are not born with all of these attributes – they're learned, they are caught, they're passed down through the generations of servicemen and women.

I might be embarrassed if anyone used those terms to describe my Christian life but I'm trying. We are in a battle of sorts, a spiritual battle. The characteristics above are no less needed in our spiritual battles. The huge advantage that we have over our enemy is that we have God on our side and he is ready and willing to equip us to fight this battle. We simply have to sign-up first, though.

I am praying that you will join me and many others in aiming to live our lives for Christ in this way, to love God with complete and total commitment. At whatever stage, you are at in your Christian journey, you can join us –

- believe in him with all of your heart
- worship him with all of our soul
- know him with all of your mind
- serve him with all of your strength

Imprint this verse on your heart, wear it on your sleeve, tie it around your head, paint it on your doorposts (see Deuteronomy 6) - whatever you do, love God wholeheartedly.

> "Love the Lord your God with all of your heart, with all of your soul, with all of your mind and with all of your strength."
>
> Mark 12:30

ABOUT SPUR CHRISTIAN PROJECTS

SPUR Christian Projects has been set up to

- spur Christians on to love and good deeds
- encourage, challenge and support Christians to spur one another on

LTLYG is the first project that has been undertaken.

If this book has prompted a response in you, please let us know. If you have experiences or thoughts on how we can spur Christians on, tell us.

You can email us at

hello@spurprojects.org.uk